ALL
ABOUT
MYTHS

AMERICAN INDIAN
MYTHS AND
LEGENDS

Catherine Chambers

Raintree
Chicago, Illinois

To contact Capstone Global Library, please
call 800-747-4992, or visit our web site,
www.capstonepub.com

Edited by Nancy Dickmann and Abby Colich
Designed by Jo Hinton-Malivoire
Original illustrations © Capstone Global Library
    Ltd 2013
Illustrations by Xöul
Picture research by Elizabeth Alexander
Production by Victoria Fitzgerald
Originated by Capstone Global Library Ltd
Printed and bound in China by China Translation
    and Printing Services

17 16 15 14 13
10 9 8 7 6 5 4 3 2 1

**Library of Congress Cataloging-in-
Publication Data**
Chambers, Catherine, 1954-
    American Indian stories and legends / Catherine
Chambers.—1 [edition].
        p. cm.—(All about myths)
    Includes bibliographical references and index.
    ISBN 978-1-4109-5469-5—ISBN 978-1-4109-
5475-6 (pbk.) 1. Indian mythology—North
America. 2. Indians of North America—Folklore.
I. Title.

E98.R3 .C632013
398.2089'97—dc23   2012043974

Acknowledgments
We would like to thank the following for
permission to reproduce photographs:
We would like to thank the following for
permission to reproduce photographs:
Alamy: pp. 9 (© Don Klumpp), 14 (© Flame), 15 (©
FLPA), 24 (© WorldFoto), 35 (© PJF); Bridgeman:
pp. 21 (© Chicago History Museum, USA), 25
(© Look and Learn); Corbis: pp. 5 (© Carolina
Biological/Visuals Unlimited), 12 (© Bettmann), 39
(© Corbis), 41 (© Kevin P. Casey); Getty Images:
pp. 6 (Jemal Countess/WireImage), 8 (Marilyn
Angel Wynn/Nativestock), 20 (Transcendental
Graphics/Archive Photos), 26 (Michael Courtney/
Warner Bros.), 28 (Werner Forman/Universal
Images Group), 33 (John Weinstein/Field
Museum Library); Rex Features: p. 40 (Everett
Collection); Shutterstock: pp. 13 (© Dee Golden),
27 (© Kenneth Keifer), 29 (© Peter Waters);
Superstock: pp. 7 (Universal Images Group), 19
(Mike Grandmaison / All Canada Photos), 32 (Tips
Images), 34 (Fotosearch), 38 (Carver Mostardi /
age fotostock); The Art Archive: p. 18 (Gianni Dagli
Orti).

Design features: Shutterstock: (© Vangelis76, © B
& T Media Group Inc., © welcomia, © Manamana,
© pashabo, © Vladislav Gurfinkel, © IrinaK, ©
nienora, © Lukiyanova Natalia / frenta).

Cover photo of cedar totum pole carved by Tony
Hunt of the Kwakiuti Nation reproduced with
permission from Photoshot (© Craig Lovell).
Background image reproduced with permission
from Shutterstock (© Martin Capek).

The publishers would like to thank Dr. Scott
Manning Stevens for his invaluable assistance in
the production of this book.

Every effort has been made to contact copyright
holders of any material reproduced in this book.
Any omissions will be rectified in subsequent
printings if notice is given to the publisher.

CONTENTS

Did you know?

Discover some interesting facts about American Indian stories.

WHO'S WHO?

Find out more about some of the main characters in American Indian stories.

MYTH LINKS

Learn about similar characters or stories from other cultures.

LAND OF MYTH AND LEGEND

The vast plains, mountains, creeks, and forests of the United States and Canada are home to 2.5 million American Indians from well over 1,000 tribes. Their countless myths and legends explain and praise both the beauty and danger of nature and the land.

MYTH OR LEGEND?

Myths and legends help make sense of the world around us. Myths are ancient tales of creation, migration, conflict, beasts, plants, and spirit powers that we cannot see. They explain and guide our behavior and our relationships.

Legends tell tales of real people, creatures, or events of the past. Over time, mystical happenings have been woven into true history. Myths and legends are handed down through the generations by word of mouth, writings, music, dance, or artworks.

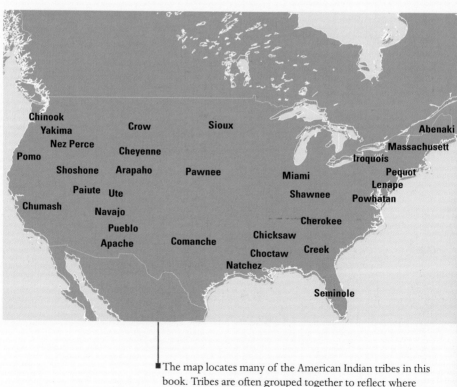

■The map locates many of the American Indian tribes in this book. Tribes are often grouped together to reflect where they live, such as Plains Indians and Woodland Indians.

Long ago, North America and Asia were connected by a land bridge. Thousands of years ago, ancient people migrated across it from Asia to North America. They settled across the United States and Canada. The land bridge is now submerged (underwater), under the Bering Sea. Migration myths are common in many American Indian communities.

MYTH LINKS

Vikings from Scandinavia landed in North America over 1,000 years ago—500 years before Columbus! We know this through their sagas, which are ancient legends. We also know that Vikings traded with American Indians. In one tale, the Viking trader Karlesefni and his friend, Snorri, gave red cloth in exchange for warm American Indian furs.

Many American Indian stories are linked to their ancient hunting culture. This Clovis spear design was used by hunters over 10,000

SPIRITS OF CREATION

Each American Indian tribe has its own way of explaining how the world began through creation myths and great creator spirits. Great Spirit is also known as Great Mystery, Old Man, Mother Earth, and Sky Goddess. Each creates all things in beauty and harmony. The Great Spirit also keeps order over other spirits, who inhabit both heaven and earth and are in all things, both living and human-made.

■ Dances connect people with the Great Spirit. This performance took place in New York City in 2005.

GREAT DREAMS

In Abenaki tradition, from the northeast, the Great Spirit was at first alone and saw no light or life anywhere. He asked Turtle to fill the emptiness with mountains and canyons. The Great Spirit was so tired after this that he fell asleep and dreamed of a chaotic world with flying, walking, creeping, talking birds, beasts, and humans. When he awoke, there they all were in a real and harmonious world.

WHO'S WHO?

Spider Woman is the creator spirit of the Hopi, from northern Arizona. Tawa is her partner. Together they sang the First Magic Song, which created Earth, light, and life. Tawa's thoughts transformed into birds, beasts, and humans before he soared into the sky. Spider Woman stayed on Earth, leading people to their homelands before she sank deep down through shifting sands.

This magnificent sculpture shows an American Indian appealing to the Great Spirit. The sculpture is displayed in the Museum of Fine Arts in Boston, Massachusetts.

KEEPING A
BALANCE

Myths tell how creator spirits balance good and bad in the world. They balance the weather, too, bringing sun and shade, winter and summer. As creators they are a kindly force, helping humans by giving them contrasts and choices.

TRIAL AND ERROR

But creator spirits can make mistakes! Gluskabe, of the Abenaki tribe, first created giant humans out of stone. But they were destructive, and their hearts were hard and cold. So Gluskabe broke them into small pieces and instead carved humans from an ash tree. These humans had soft hearts that were green and growing, like the inside of an ash branch.

This belt is woven with wampum, which are beads made from whelk and clam shells. Eastern woodland American Indians weave historical records on them.

WHO'S WHO?

The Iroquois of New York state tell of a Sky Woman who fell through a hole in the heavens to an Earth created by animals on the back of a turtle. Her twin grandchildren, Sapling and Flint, balanced good and bad forces. Sapling created helpful tools and battled with monsters. But Flint caused destruction.

Mythical figures such as Raven, a great creator spirit, are carved on totem poles. The poles come from the northwest coast and are made from cedar wood.

Did you know?

Myths and legends have been handed down mostly by word of mouth, or as ceremonies known as "sings." Some tribes, such as the Mi'Kmaq of Nova Scotia, developed their own writing system in pictogram form to tell the tales. The Ojibwe (from Michigan to Alberta) etched them onto birch bark and rolled them into scrolls called wiigwaasabak

The First Humans—A Natchez Myth from the Southern Mississippi

Way up in the sky, Wise Old Man was sitting on a cloud, busily designing the first humans. The first one was looking good. Suddenly a rumble interrupted him. It was Thunder.

"Oh, Great Spirit!" boomed Thunder. "When you've finished making humans, I'd like them to be mine."

Wise Old Man shook his head, "Sorry, Thunder. They can be your grandchildren if you like but concentrate on warning them when storms are coming." Thunder grumbled away just as blazing Sun rose above the clouds.

"Oh Great Spirit! Can humans be mine?" dazzled Sun.

"Not a good idea, Sun," replied Wise Old Man. "But they can be your friends and you can give them light." Sun sighed, blushed, and sank over the horizon just as Moon appeared.

"You can be uncle to the humans and glow softly so that they can see their way," advised Wise Old Man as a sudden spark flew in the dark.

"Oh, Great Spirit," crackled Fire, "please make humans be mine!"

"Not a good idea for you to get too close to humans, Fire," replied Wise Old Man. "But keep them nice and warm and cook their food."

Wind breezed in, blowing Fire out. Surely he'd be in charge of humans?

Wise Old Man shook his head, "They need you to puff away unhealthy air. And as for you, Rainbow," he continued, as colors arched above Earth, "just stop those floods!" Rainbow faded, leaving a trickle of Water.

Wise Old Man was a bit fed up by now. "Water, don't bother! Just keep humans clean and fresh."

Exhausted, Wise Old Man called out across the heavens. "Oh, Thunder, Sun, Fire, Wind, Rainbow, and Water—and anyone else! Be grateful, my servants, that I've told you how you can help humans. And never, ever forget that when I've finished making them, they'll all be MINE!"

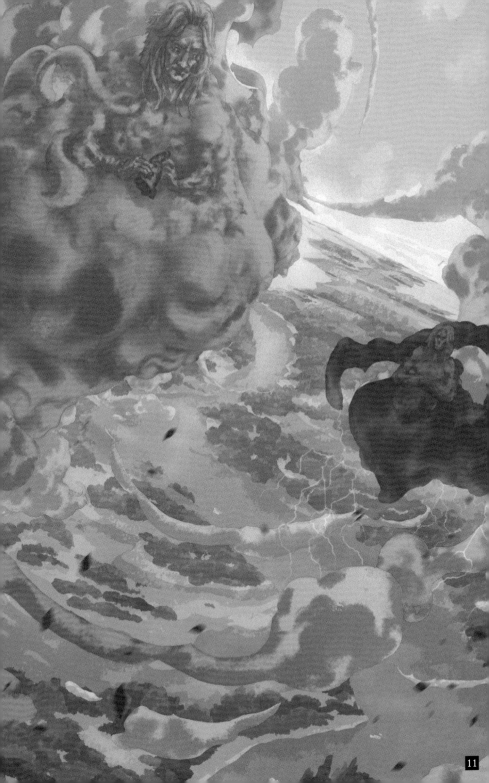

HOW CREATURES GOT THEIR FEATURES

Creation stories explain how creatures got their features. The Wabanaki are a group of tribes that include the Abenaki. They live on the eastern seashore, known as the "dawn land." One story tells of Rabbit, who once had short ears. One day, Rabbit lied to his fellow creatures that Sun would not rise the next day. They all panicked, thinking that winter was near. But Rabbit's lie got out, so he hid in fear behind a stone. Great Spirit yanked him up by his ears, which made them very long. But it didn't stop Rabbit from being a trickster, as we shall see!

Did you know?

Many American Indians use sweat lodges, which are a kind of sauna to help a person's spirit. In Ojibwe myth, the Great Spirit created sweat lodges by sending sun and wind to help an old woman's daughter give birth to the first sons on Earth. One of them was Stone Boy. The old woman heated him up and poured hot water over his stone body, creating steam and the first sweat lodge.

Sweat lodges can be made in domes of animal hides, or sunk into the earth, covered with wood and walled with stone.

A Creek myth tells how a woman washed and rubbed her feet, and from them the first corn seed grew.

WHO'S WHO?

In a Cherokee myth (from the southeast), all Earth's creatures got together to make the first pair of antlers. Deer and Rabbit competed for them in a race. Rabbit chewed a shortcut through some bushes but got caught. The other creatures were so angry, they gave the antlers to Deer.

SPIRITS EVERYWHERE

Creatures, trees, stones, rivers, birds, insects, crops, and all other parts of creation can hold a spirit inside them. Spirits help to create harmony between humans and nature. But some spirits can be destructive!

WISE EAGLES AND TERRIBLE THUNDERS

Eagles have sharp eyesight that gives them spiritual vision. They soar up high to the all-knowing spirits in the sky. This gives them great wisdom. A Pueblos myth (from the southwest) tells that they send and receive prayers and protection from the sky gods.

Thunder brings helpful rain but also destructive storms. Booming thunder is the sound of Thunderbird cracking his great wings. His eyes and beak flash with lightning!

The Achomawi from California believe that Silver Fox was created from fog and Coyote from a lumpy cloud. They became sky spirits whose very first thought changed into a useful canoe.

Did you know?

Fire is vital to American Indians, as it brings light and warmth and cooks food. So Fire Spirits are very important, but not all are good! One story tells how three Fire Spirit witches guarded the world's fire and would not let people near it. But Coyote stole a firestick from them and, with the help of other creatures, brought it to humans.

This Green Corn Festival is an ancient celebration to thank and honor the spirits of nature for a good harvest.

The Battle of the Season Spirits—A Tale of the Acoma from the Southwest

Long ago, the Acoma people built their first settlement, White City. The city's governor had a daughter, Cochinnenako, who was married to Shakok, the northern Spirit of Winter. Shakok brought bitter weather and starvation, for corn could not ripen in the freezing cold.

One day, Cochinnenako went out to gather spiky cactus leaves, which was the only food around. She was alone, as her husband had gone north to play with icicles.

Suddenly a man appeared dressed in bright yellow and green clothes, and carrying an ear of corn.

"Are you really eating cactus leaves?" asked the stranger. "Here, take this corn to your family. I'll bring more tomorrow from my home in the warm south."

"Oh, please take me home with you," pleaded Cochinnenako. "My husband Shakok is so, so cold."

"No! He'd be furious!" replied the traveler quickly. So Cochinnenako walked home sadly.

"Cheer up," said her father. "Your stranger is Miochin, the Spirit of the warm South."

The next day, Miochin brought enough corn to feed the whole city. But that evening, Shakok breezed in. At the sight of hot Miochin, his icy body melted, revealing only dried, bleached rushes.

"I will gather an army and then you'll be sorry!" shouted the embarrassed Shakok.

Shakok returned, bringing all the creatures of the North to help him, with Magpie as his shield,

"Here! This'll wipe the smile off your face!" shouted Shakok, belting Miochin with lightning. But behind a wall of fire and smoke, with the leathery-skinned Bat as his shield, Miochin stood firm. Shakok and his army were soon sitting miserably in pools of water.

"Look, I tell you what," said Miochin kindly. "Let's share the year, half can be Winter and half Summer."

Now, the Spirit of Winter doesn't smile often, but at this, he did.

SHAMANS

Spirits can guide you, but how do you reach them? Shamans are healers with powers to link ordinary people to the spirit world. They use trances, medicinal herbs, fasting, and drumming. They also help find a sacred, remote spot where a person receives guidance through a vision quest. This is a spiritual journey that lasts for several days and ends in amazing visions that a shaman explains.

PIPE DREAMS

Smoking a sacred tobacco pipe helps adults to reach the spirits. According to Sioux myth, White Buffalo Woman appeared in a vision to two leaders, telling them that she would teach them seven ceremonies. These would help them interact with the spirit world. They included tobacco pipe rituals and the vision quest. After teaching them, she disappeared, leaving behind a sacred bundle of secret objects, which is kept on a Sioux reservation to this day.

The Kwakwaka'wakw of British Columbia celebrate generous spirits of nature at the potlatch ceremony of giving to family and neighboring tribes. They hold it in lodges like this one.

Did you know?

Lake Manitoba is a large lake in Canada. *Manitou* means "spirit" in Algonquian. *Manitoba* refers to the place where the waters narrow, "the spirit straits."

Teaching children to respect the spirits of nature is known as the "way of truth" or "the way of beauty" among the Navajo of New Mexico. Other tribes, such as the Hopi, call it "the red road." The red road is a safe, respectful, and healthy way to raise children and is very similar to the "rightful path" of the Chinese Tao religion.

HEROES AND VILLAINS

Many American Indian legends are based on real events in history. The Wabenaki tell how they heroically tried to fend off the Vikings with their magical bow. Since then, there have been many real-life heroes and heroines. Many of the tales about them are tinged with the supernatural.

THE STORY OF SITTING BULL

Sitting Bull, of the Lakota people, was famous for predicting the defeat of the U.S. army under General Custer at the Battle of Little Bighorn in 1876. The legend tells how Sitting Bull's supernatural powers as a holy man and healer helped him to predict the victory. He was at first called a name that means "slow." But wisdom is not thought to come quickly, which is why elders are so respected.

Each feather in a headdress represents a warrior or chief's brave deed and reminds them of the legendary story behind it.

MYTH LINKS

Nearly 200 years ago in southern Africa, Shaka became the mighty King of the Zulu people. He invented a lethal short spear, or "ixlwa," which was thought to have magical strength. He gave his soldiers long, leather "ishlangu" shields, believed to give special powers of protection.

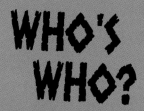

WHO'S WHO?

Once, there was a young man from the Eastern Woodlands Sauk tribe who did not start off as a chief. But he inherited a sacred medicine bundle, and through its mysterious spirit he became a heroic war leader of his people. He became known as Black Hawk (1767–1838) and led the Sauk and the Fox tribes against settlers in Illinois and Wisconsin.

The Hero and the Horned Snakes— A Cherokee Myth

Once, long ago, there were enormous two-horned snakes that glistened and slithered among towering rocks above the land of the Cherokee. The snakes were so bright they dazzled anyone who tried to hunt them. Their evil magic pulled people toward them before they gobbled them up.

Only very clever medicine men managed to kill them. Or champion hunters who could shoot an arrow through the seventh stripe of the snake's skin.

One day, a band of Cherokee captured a young man from the Shawnee tribe.

"You're staying here to work for us," they said. "That is, unless you can find and kill a two-horned snake!" They roared with mocking laughter.

The young Shawnee hunter quietly left for the hills with his bow and arrows, followed at a safe distance by the Cherokee. He climbed over rocks and searched deep inside caves. Then, high in the Tennessee Mountains, he spied a two-horned snake, smiling cruelly with his slimy mouth.

Our brave hunter created a ring of dried pine cones and set fire to them with his fire stick. Then he walked toward the snake.

"Freedom or death!" cried the Shawnee. He shot an arrow straight through the seventh stripe of the furious snake then jumped safely inside the ring of fire. Dark, inky poison oozed out of the dying snake.

The Cherokee were amazed. "You have earned your freedom, brave Shawnee!" they cried.

After four days, some of the Cherokee returned to the spot where the mighty snake was slain.

"This is now a place of magic," said one. "Let's gather the snake's dried skin and bones and tie them in a bundle to protect our children and grandchildren."

A small lake of inky water formed where the snake died. Here, Cherokee women learned to dye their woven baskets, by dipping them until they turned as black as the snake's blood.

HEROES OF NATURE

Some heroic nature spirits fight for humans, some help each other out, while others seek justice for themselves. One Wabanaki story tells of the heroic Partridge Wizard spirit. He won a fierce battle with evil porcupine magicians after they killed his wife.

WISE GRANDMOTHER WOODCHUCK

Wisdom can be heroic and is greatly prized. It is used in dangerous situations to save the natural world from disaster. Grandmother Woodchuck, another Wabanaki spirit, often steers the kindly monster, Gluskabe, away from creating chaos for humans.

Gluskabe is a feisty fighter of mighty beasts and evil spirits. He means well, but he doesn't always think things through. Once he tied up a scary giant eagle but forgot that Eagle makes the wind blow around the world. Gluskabe only untied him after Grandmother Woodchuck remarked that without wind, the world would be hot and airless and it would bring disease to nature.

The heroic Ojibwe weasel-like spirit called the Great Fisher fights monsters and brings summer to the world. Afterward, he becomes the Big Dipper constellation.

MYTH LINKS

In China, fierce dragons are also a force for good. In myth, the dragon first appeared above a new-born Chinese emperor, bringing good fortune to the boy and his country. This dragon also controls the weather and the waters. He often appears in festivals with a pearl symbol, which helped people's wishes to be granted.

The Choctaw of the southern Mississippi perform dance-songs called hitla tutuwa. Some hitla tutuwa enact the powerful characters of spirit creatures, such as Turtle, Duck, Beaver, Turkey, Racoon, Quail, and even tiny Gnat. The Choctaw also had their own version of the native stickball game, which the French called lacrosse.

CHILLING TALES

Horrifying villains bring terror to American Indian tales. For example, wicked Wendigo is a scary monster giant who is greedy and eats people for fun. This northeastern character is often covered in ice. Where his heart should be, there lies a human. If you kill a Wendigo, then you usually kill the human inside, too.

CHILLY CHENOO

Mi'kmaq myths tell of Chenoo, an ice monster. He is skinny, has large fangs, and his power rests in a human form made of ice and lodged in his stomach. If you can make Chenoo vomit the ice man, then the ice man will become a real human and Chenoo will lose his strength. Chopping up a Chenoo into little pieces is the best way to kill him. Or you could get him to swallow a salt lump to melt his insides.

Did you know?

American Indian stories and tales make us think about our behavior. Wendigo appears greedy and selfish, but if someone wants to kill him, they also have to kill the human inside. Through Wendigo tales, we learn to think before we act. On the other hand, sacrifices sometimes have to be made for the good of others. Nothing is simple!

A Wendigo is a demon who possesses and transforms people. Sometimes he is depicted with antlers and long claws. In myth, he lives on his own in the remote wilderness.

WHO'S WHO?

In Hopi myth, Kwa'koto was part man, part eagle. He whisked young women up into the clouds and ate them. Kwa'koto snatched the good Son of Light's wife. But a pinyon tree (below) spirit gave the Son of Light sticky resin to make a false coat of armor for Kwa'koto. The armor melted, leaving the monster defenseless.

CUNNING TRICKSTERS

Many myths feature trickster characters. Tricksters try to cheat their enemies, and even their friends, to get what they want. Trickster tales always have a twist in them and a message. Some tricksters are shape-shifting spirits that can change from animals to humans or trees.

Some, like Raven, are famous creators, but there are also stories where Raven shows his cunning. For example, one day he was hungry and spied Whale out on the ocean. He tricked Whale into opening his mouth and then jumped in. Taking a knife, he hacked off whale's meat and cooked it over a fire. When Whale's body floated ashore, some fishermen opened up Whale and Raven hopped out.

This is a Haida tribal rattle in the shape of Raven, the trickster and creator. He stole the sunlight and brought it to his people.

MYTH LINKS

Tricksters feature in the myths of many cultures. For example, Anansi is the spider trickster of West Africa's Ashanti people. Anansi runs along his sticky threads between Nyame, the creator sky god, and earthly beings. African slaves took Anansi to the Americas, where he became "Aunt Nancy."

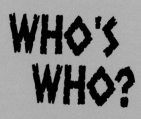

■ Spiders feature in many tales and are also real-life tricksters. The Black Widow spider tricks her prey into her web.

WHO'S WHO?

In Creek myth, Rabbit complains to the Great Life Controller, "When I get attacked by other creatures, all I can do is run." So Life Controller asks him to fetch a Rattlesnake and a swarm of Gnats. Through wits and trickery, Rabbit ties up Rattlesnake and bags the Gnats. "See?" says Life Controller. "You don't just have fast legs, you have brains, too!"

Coyote's Fishy Tale—A Klamath Myth from California

One hot day, hungry Coyote wandered by the great Klamath River, high up in the California desert.

"Mmm!" he exclaimed suddenly, sniffing the air. "Sumptuous, sizzling salmon! Must be lunch time for those two lucky girls—the guardians of all the salmon in the world. And they only take one salmon at a time for themselves! What a waste. I'll pay them a visit and change all that!"

First, Coyote hacked off a piece of bark from an alder tree and whittled it into the shape of a salmon. Then he smeared it with a deer's red marrow fat to give it some color.

"Hi there!" said Coyote cheerfully, as he approached the girls. The girls knew Coyote's tricksy ways, so they quickly gobbled up their crispy-skinned salmon.

Coyote smiled, but to the girls' horror, took out his fake fish and hoisted it on two sticks over the fire. They looked at each other, both thinking the same thing. Coyote must have stolen it!

"When we get a chance, we must check the salmon trap!" they whispered.

Coyote turned his back on the girls and made chomping noises on the fake fish. Then he lay down and pretended to sleep, waiting for the girls to leave camp and lead him to the salmon trap.

Now, fish is very good for the brain. So the two smart girls tested to see if Coyote was really asleep by burning the end of his tail with a roaring fire. But Coyote bit his lip and stayed still. Then he followed the girls toward the river.

"The trap's fine," they shrugged, and made their way home.

"Wahey, it's my day!" cried Coyote, pouncing on the trap. But then, "NOOO!" For Coyote flung back the lid so wide that all the salmon escaped down into the rivers of the whole world. And Coyote never did catch one!

By the way, we now also know why Coyote has a scorched black stripe on his tail!

TRICKY HUMANS

Humans are often the tricksters' victims. But sometimes, it's humans who trick the monsters! For example, in Iroquois myth, a terrifying monster head with no body hurls through the air toward an old lady who's warming herself by the fire. She sees him coming and starts chewing on some roasted chestnuts. Head-monster thinks she's eating stones that are being heated by the fireside. He puts the stones in his mouth, starts chomping on them, and burns himself up.

■ Paul Bunyan is standing with his companion, Babe the Blue Ox. Unlike American Indians, Paul Bunyan didn't understand the importance of conserving forests and creatures.

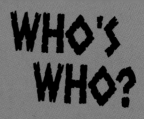

WHO'S WHO?

Nanabozho is a mild shape-shifting trickster of the northeast who is more cheeky than bad. He often does something unexpected. He appears in the tale of mythical super lumberjack Paul Bunyan, who cut down too many trees and spoiled the natural forest. Nanabozho fought Bunyan for 40 days and then surprised him by aiming a Red Lake Walleye fish at him, which killed him.

Did you know?

Fossil hunters believe that some monster shape-shifters were real prehistoric beasts. The Shoshone tell stories of a monster bull with a flat nose, sharp shiny horns, and enormous teeth. Archaeologists have found fossils of a giant flat-nosed bear from Alaska down to New Mexico. Could this be the same creature?

DEATH AND THE AFTERLIFE

How did death happen? In Sioux beliefs, the Great Spirit asked the first woman on Earth to pick up either buffalo dung or a stone to throw into a pool of water. She chose the stone, which of course sank. And that's why all living things sink into death in the end.

For American Indians, the land can get sick and die, too. A Mother Earth dance helps to restore the land's spirits.

BENEATH THE EARTH

There are many traditions and myths surrounding burial. Among the Navajo, mourners bury a person four days after they die. They leave by a different path from the one they carried the body along, and cover all footprints in case the spirit of the dead person follows them.

BEYOND THE GRAVE

Among most American Indian cultures, the spirit never dies, but moves into a different stage, state, or place. Spirits can be reincarnated and come back to Earth as other people, birds, or beasts—or even a tree. Some change into a ghost.

Among herdsmen and hunters, the spirit might find itself in a beautiful heaven full of deer, buffalo, or moose—a happy hunting ground. For farmers the spirit can make its way to a lush, green underworld ruled by Mother Earth.

MYTH LINKS

The Sami people live in a chilly land called Sápmi, which stretches across Scandinavia and part of Russia. Here, many Sami tend their reindeer herds. Like American Indian herding cultures, they believe heaven has hundreds of healthy deer and large patches of delicious cloudberries.

Carved wooden prayer sticks are plunged into the ground at burial sites. They link the living to the world of the dead.

The Fireball Ghost—A Maliseet Myth of the Northeast

Deep in the darkening woods, two hunters stood still, gazing in every direction.

"We're definitely lost, and night is falling," said one, shaking his head. "But the trees look a little thinner in the east, so maybe there's a clearing where we can set up camp."

They walked ahead and found not just a clearing, but a lodge.

"Phew! The spirits are with us!" said the other hunter. "We'd have frozen to death out here."

The two hunters pushed open the door, made a fire, and took out some dried moose meat from a pouch.

"Let's get some sleep on those two soft fir-branch bunk beds in the corner. We'll find our way back in the morning," said one. Suddenly, his friend screamed, for in one of the bunks lay a dead man.

"Stop screaming!" snapped the first hunter. "Help me get rid of him and then we'll bunk down."

During the night, the second hunter was awoken by a chilling gurgling sound. The dead stranger was sucking the blood out of his friend's neck! The hunter kicked the door wide open and ran as fast as he could, with a horrifying ghostly "WHOOOO!" noise following him.

He could feel the great fireball ghost of the dead stranger roaring after him. At last, he saw his village and collapsed into his house.

"What happened?" cried his neighbors, and they gathered to listen to the hunter's terrible tale. A shaman and a group of the strongest men then made their way to the lodge, where the dead stranger lay with blood all around his mouth. Their dead friend's neck was chewed to pieces.

They carried their friend away.

"Now burn that place down to the ground!" ordered the shaman.

As the flames soared, the lodge's blazing roof fell in. One final, chilling "WHOOOO!" pierced the air as the great ghostly ball of fire disappeared high above the clouds into the afterlife.

REACHING THE AFTERLIFE

There are many different beliefs about the afterlife and how to reach it. A shaman's prayers can guide the spirit. But a dead person might have to walk a balance beam to weigh the good and bad in their life. Mourners might burn cedarwood or sage leaves, or smoke a pipe to help the spirit on its way.

■ American Indians might be left outside or buried in a place of natural beauty when they die. A large mound marks the spot, like this site in Illinois.

SEARCHING FOR LOST SOULS

Some afterlife myths describe quests to find the spirits of the dead. For example, an Algonquian tale tells of a young man who has lost the love of his life. He seeks her out in the land of the dead. There, he finds her blissfully happy in a beautiful place, but he knows he must return to Earth. The quest is actually a dream, but he knows that one day they will meet again.

MYTH LINKS

In ancient Persia's Zoroastrian culture, the dead walk over a bridge no thicker than a hair to reach the afterlife. The Scandinavian Norse bridge shakes if the person isn't ready to die. According to Chinese tradition, your whole life is judged along the length of the bridge: all your thoughts, words, and actions.

Some American Indians prefer not to be buried on or under the ground. This is a Plains Indian burial platform, on which the corpse is placed.

MYTHS AND LEGENDS
ALIVE

In myth and in life, American Indians pledge respect for each other and the earth. Their myths encourage us to cherish nature. In life, American Indians have been at the forefront of conservation for over 300 years. But myths are also fun and have inspired some great modern fictional characters!

Another artist, Jack Kirby, took many heroes and villains from American Indian mythology and made them into film stars. There's the great Spiderman and Spiderwoman, the X-Men's Beast Boy based on Hopi mythology, the Ojibwe's Ice Man, and many more.

HEROES AND VILLAINS OF OUR TIME

Cartoon characters Wile E. Coyote and Road Runner, whom he chases and tries to trick, are based on American Indian characters. They were brought to life 65 years ago by the cartoon creator, Chuck Jones.

■ Road Runner, like mythical American Indian characters, uses magic to outwit his rivals. He crashes through paintings of scenery into a new landscape to escape them.

This is a caucus, a political meeting in the United States. Many believe that the caucus comes from an Algonquian word and idea for "counsel."

Did you know?

Ancient American Indian myths urge us to live in harmony with the planet. Modern political movements give the same message. Remember the story of Coyote and the salmon (see pages 30–31)? Today, the Klamath tribe campaign against dams on the upper reaches of the river, which they claim stop the salmon from migrating and breeding downstream.

WHO'S WHO?

Agnes Yellowknee is an American Indian librarian who has built a tribal library in her tree house. The library contains oral traditions that have now been written down, including myths and legends. There are also modern stories with ancient mythical traditions at their core.

CHARACTERS
AND
CREATURES

CHARACTERS

Black Hawk legendary 19th-century leader of the Sauk tribe

Cochinnenako mythical daughter of the first governor of the Acoma tribe. She is married to Shakok.

Coyote trickster spirit, sky spirit, and much more! He belongs to many tribes.

Eagle wise sky spirit of many tribes

Flint unhelpful twin grandson of Iroquois Sky woman spirit

Gluskabe Abenaki and other Algonquian-speaking tribes' great creator spirit and monster

Grandmother Woodchuck a wise spirit of the Algonquian tribes who guides Gluskabe, a creator monster

Great Fisher heroic Ojibwe weasel-like spirit that fights monsters

Great Spirit great creator for many tribes, with many different names

Miochin Warm Spirit of Summer of the Acoma people

Partridge Wizard a heroic spirit that wins a fierce battle against an evil porcupine magician

Paul Bunyan a mythical superman lumberjack who cuts down a lot of trees

Rabbit trickster of many American Indian tribes

Sapling helpful twin grandson of Iroquois Sky woman spirit

Shakok Spirit of Winter of the Acoma tribe. He is married to Cochinnenako.

Silver Fox animal sky spirit of the Achomwi tribe

Sitting Bull legendary 19th-century chief of the Lakota Sioux tribe

Son of Light good spirit of the Hopi tribe, who defeats Kwa'koto

Spider Woman a heroic creator spirit from the Hopi and other tribes

Stone Boy the first son of the Ojibwe tribe's Great Spirit. The stone son became the first sweat lodge.

Thunderbird powerful storm spirit of many tribes

White Buffalo Woman powerful mythical spirit who teaches spiritual connections to the Sioux tribes

Wise Old Man great creator spirit of the Natchez and other tribes

CREATURES

Chenoo chilly ice monster from the Mi'kmaq tribe

Kwa'koto Man Eagle monster of the Hopi

Nanabozho a mild, shape-shifting trickster of the northeast

Windigo wicked, greedy northeastern monster giant with a human as his heart

GLOSSARY

balance beam beam that a dead person walks along. It weighs the good and bad in a person's life.

birch bark bark of the birch tree

buffalo dung buffalo poop

cloudberry favorite berry in Scandinavia that looks a bit like a raspberry

Clovis North American culture of 13,500 years ago. Hunters made a particular style of flint spearheads during this time, called a Clovis point.

constellation pattern of bright stars that are close to each other

etch carve or score using a sharp instrument

fasting not eating for a while in order to achieve a spiritual goal

hitla tutuwa dance song that enacts powerful characters of spirit creatures

manitou name for spirit in many American Indian languages

marrow core of fat and blood inside a bone

pictogram drawn or carved symbol that looks like the idea or object it represents. Pictograms can be read to tell a myth.

pinyon pine tree that produces resin and edible nuts

Potlatch ceremony of giving to family and neighboring tribes

prayer stick decorated stick that is set into the earth to link the living with the spirit of a person who has died

reincarnation returning to life on Earth after death, sometimes in a different form

saga long story about the history of a family, or a myth or legend of Scandinavian and other Germanic peoples of northern Europe

shaman spiritual and physical healer

shape-shifting changing from one form to another. It could be anything from a ghost to a bear, or a human to an eagle.

sing ceremony of words and music that tells myths and traditions

stickball traditional American Indian team game using long sticks and a ball. It was often played to settle disputes. The game of lacrosse comes from it.

sweat lodge type of sauna. It is a hot, steamy room used to cleanse the mind and spirit, as well as the body.

totem pole tall pole made of red cedar wood and carved with symbols and creatures, including mythical figures. Totem poles are symbols of family and tribal unity.

trance sleep-like state in which a person sees visions

Vision Quest when a person is taken to a quiet, sacred place to achieve a spiritual vision. A shaman helps the person through different steps to attain the dream.

wampum beads made from whelk or clam shells. They are made into belts or used to decorate other clothing. Histories can be depicted on wampum belts.

FIND OUT MORE

BOOKS

Dembicki, Matt. *Trickster: Native American Tales: A Graphic Collection.* Golden, Colo.: Fulcrum Publishing, 2010.

Goble, Paul. *The Earth Made New: Plains Indian Stories of Creation.* Bloomington, Ind.: World Wisdom, 2009.

Murdoch, David S. *North American Indian.* New York: DK Children, 2005.

Schoolcraft, Henry R. *The Enchanted Moccasins and Other Native American Legends.* Mineola, N.Y.: Dover Publications, 2007.

Wood, Marion, and Andy Mathis. *Native American Civilizations.* New York: Rosen, 2009.

WEB SITES

www.indigenouspeople.net/stories.htm

Learn more about stories of native peoples from around North America and other parts of the world.

www.nmai.si.edu/searchcollections/home.aspx

You can explore the collection of the National Museum of the American Indian at this page from their web site.

publications.newberry.org/indiansofthemidwest

Past and present American Indians of the Midwest are explored on this web site.

www.wwu.edu/skywise/legends.html

This web site tells a lot about mythical characters, as well as American Indian culture.

PLACES TO VISIT

National Museum of the American Indian
Washington, DC
New York, New York
Suitland, Maryland
nmai.si.edu/home
The National Museum of the American Indian (NMAI) is part
of the Smithsonian Institution. It includes three locations: the
museum on the National Mall in Washington, DC; the George
Gustav Heye Center (GGHC) in New York City; and the Cultural
Resources Center (CRC) in Suitland, Maryland. The collections
of the NMAI include objects, photographs, archives, and media
covering the entire Western Hemisphere.

Mitchell Museum of the American Indian
Evanston, Illinois
www.mitchellmuseum.org/index.html
The Mitchell Museum of the American Indian is devoted to the
history, culture, and arts of the American Indian and First Nation
peoples of the United States and Canada.

FURTHER RESEARCH

If you enjoyed a particular story in this book, you could draw a
picture of it or make a model of one of the characters. There are
often no descriptions of some of the characters and spirits. So try
to use the pictures in the book, the web sites listed here, and the
meaning of the story to help you imagine how they would look.

INDEX